"Kerry James Evans mines his own experience, and with each poem unboxes honest feelings. His rules are simple: make sense, sing without pretension, take chances, imagine, reveal. The wonder is that he never seems to strain as he fights for that impossible understanding, poetry. *Nine Persimmons* is a major victory."

　　—RODNEY JONES, author of *Salvation Blues* and *Alabama*

"'I play it out measure by measure,' writes Kerry James Evans. And those soulful measures are filled with a music that is unabashedly Southern. These poems are haunted, full of grit, and down-home. They have no quit in them. If the great Harry Crews had written poetry, he might have written something like Evans's *Nine Persimmons*."

　　—TOMÁS Q. MORÍN, author of *Machete* and *Patient Zero*

"How does a poet write if an eight-year-old heart still knocks in his chest? A child peers out a car window and beckons to the moon, 'Come to me, Moon.' In Kerry James Evans's *Nine Persimmons* the moon conspires, and the sun, the crack in the living room wall, pelicans, guitars, a bag of ice, a French horn, and even God all deliver. The tone, longing. In an honest voice born from a hardscrabble childhood rich with love and labor, Evans gives us a book of 'peanuts and Coca-Cola and a sprinkling of New Testament.' A book of struggle where here, in rural Georgia, 'is the heaven of Paradisio.'"

　　—ALICE FRIMAN, author of *On the Overnight Train: New and Selected Poems*

The
Backwaters
Press

The Backwaters Prize in Poetry Honorable Mention

Nine Persimmons

Kerry James Evans

The Backwaters Press
An imprint of the University of Nebraska Press

For customers in the EU with safety/GPSR concerns, contact:
gpsr@mare-nostrum.co.uk
Mare Nostrum Group BV
Mauritskade 21D
1091 GC Amsterdam
The Netherlands

Library of Congress Cataloging-in-Publication Data
Names: Evans, Kerry James author
Title: Nine persimmons / Kerry James Evans.
Other titles: Nine persimmons (Compilation)
Description: Lincoln: The Backwaters Press, an imprint of the University of Nebraska Press, 2026. | Series: The Backwaters Prize in Poetry honorable mention
Identifiers: LCCN 2025038028
ISBN 9781496243713 paperback
ISBN 9781496246035 epub
ISBN 9781496246042 pdf
Subjects: BISAC: POETRY / American / General | LCGFT: Autobiographical poetry
Classification: LCC PS3605.V36824 N56 2026 | DDC 811/.6—dc23/eng/20250905
LC record available at https://lccn.loc.gov/2025038028

Set in Adobe Garamond Pro by A. Shahan.

For Rodney Jones, James Kimbrell, and Travis Mossotti.

Contents

III

Nine Persimmons

The Heavens Opened, and God Said,

All endings, even mine, will be yours.
Take the Chevrolet Camaro—
a popular car in Florida.
Not only will Florida cease

to exist, but so will every
yellow Camaro double-parked
in a roped-off field outside
the nearest fall festival

with its haunted corn maze
and pumpkin patch—
its local AC/DC cover band
reuniting for one last tour.

Fear not, my child. Those songs
live on. They carry like bubbles
drawn from a soapy wand.
You are like a branch

that has forgotten the trunk,
a bird in a lightning storm,
waves lingering at the shore.
I am sand. I am the wave, the wind,

the red flag whipping a blue sky.
Would you believe me if I said
you and I are both blue sky?
Would you try? Do you ever

wonder what frustrates me?
Never-ending guitar solos,
legalese, and skinny pawn brokers.
Do you hear the guitar solo?

What about the neighbor's kids
burning donuts in deserted
quarries? Their bare-chested
howl is a hymn all its own.

Once, the universe was a series
of wheels within wheels. Now,
it is a shattered urn. In the beginning,
it *was* good—in the beginning.

I

The World

My parents were married in the living room of my uncle's trailer with me
    still
in my mother's womb. My mother, with her new license, loved Dolly Parton
    and roller skating.

She was sixteen. My father, eighteen, both scared out of their minds,
    ignorant of a world
beyond their high school districts—beyond "big towns" like Birmingham
    or Tuscaloosa—*Roll Tide.*

Shit. It was 1983. Trickle-down economics, cocaine, and bull markets.
    Reagan,
the U.S. Embassy bombing in Beirut, sixty-three dead the invasion of Grenada,
    the release

of *Return of the Jedi*, because Lord knows what this world needs
    is a robed brat
with father issues wielding a laser. What do I know? I was conceived
    in the back seat

of a '66 Ford Falcon—a car I restored in high school, now retired
    to a junkyard
in northern Virginia after two divorces and a suicide attempt,
    but who cares

about a car? A sophomore, my mother carried me into a school at full term
    and learned
how to look down, but who cares about how mean kids can be?
    What awful things

they said to her. My father would join the Air Force to
    get her out of there—
they would try to *make it work*, but fail to *make it work*. They were kids
    taking on the impossible.

I would attend eight schools K–12, reside in more than twenty-seven domiciles,
    never once
calling one *home*—would learn *friends* is a name for people you must forget.
    Look at me now

—a thirty-eight-year-old revolver loaded in the glove box.
    Open it.
Look at my father's hands around my neck. Look at his father's hands
    around his.

Look how hungry I still am, how confused—how I am a country
    tearing itself
to pieces in a C-store parking lot. What do I even know? My poor mother
    still sixteen—

McDonald's three, four times a week, no retirement, obese,
    votes
for a party controlled by billionaires—yet I call her once a week, tell her
    I love you, and I do.

I love my father, who can't write a sentence, but commands troops
    in the Army—
who will retire any day now, and I love you, reader, who knows so little about me
    —who tries not to,

but can't help but judge me for how I say these things so casually—
    how my drawl
reappears like azalea blossoms in spring, then *poof!*
    Gone with the first rain.

The Photograph | Boy in Window

I know this boy
sitting on a radiator
        in front of an opened window.

This boy, sitting on a radiator
in a pair of overalls,
        legs crossed over

a patch of light
cut into the floor. I know
        this boy, whose shadow

rests on the patch of light
cut into the floor, this
        boy sitting on a radiator in a room

with no pictures
on the walls—no table,
        no chairs—no furniture

of any kind,
and I know this look,
        this longing. He's looking at me now.

He wants to speak.
It's spring and he's sitting
        on a radiator in front

of an opened window.
Outside, a bird in a gutter,
        two trees, what appears to be a house,

a rail, another window,
another bird, but the boy
        isn't looking outside.

He's sitting on a radiator
looking into the camera,
    at me, his mouth

    clenched around a word
he has yet to learn—a word
    he will never find.

    Even now,
he seems to know this,
    his legs crossed, almost swinging,

    one hand
on the sill, the other
    resting on his lap.

A Bit of Luck

Ithaca's never *that* far away, if given time and a bit of luck—
if born into royalty, chauffeured to a private school

where one's cunning is bound within a scroll containing
lessons from the trivium—of logical expansion, dilemmas,

and linguistic fallacies and fallacies of misdirection.
O, philosopher-kings of old. O, silver-threaded curtains

and crowns of gold. And I thought I was lucky to be born
in Alabama, to have been afforded a public education

from underpaid teachers who toked up on Saturday
to praise Jesus on Sunday—the best kind of teacher, the ones

who made us read closely, who introduced books
like Plato's *Republic* and sent us to the principal when we

talked over the lecture—whose paddle bore six holes
and an ergonomic handle. It's one thing to read, another

to let it sink in. These teachers knew enough of the world,
knew most of us were doomed to the trailer plant or the vfw.

One of us might manage a Pizza Hut, the other a Food Lion.
And sure, many might go to college, but most would stay,

would graduate—fewer would learn how to pray. O, rulers
of back-road, landlocked hollers. O, kingdom come.

To be born a king with a ship, a crew, who'd not only fight
by your side for a decade, but tie you to the ship's mast,

stuff wax in their ears and row the Aegean, and all of it for you
to hear the Siren's call. O, to be a king! To forget about home

for a season—to be a lotus eater! What I wouldn't give
to live with such reason, to saunter on home after a decade

at sea, to have a bow and to know how to string it, then shoot it
like a good ol' boy who steps from a jacked-up pickup and reclaims

his kingdom by firing an arrow through twelve axe handles,
then gives the nod to Penelope, who, still unconvinced,

riddles him about their bedchamber. What marriage is perfect?
Trials to be sure. Hard work, no doubt, but still, quite a bit

of luck, no? To have two sons! To have a wife who'd stay faithful
after twenty years—who'd take you back? After my one

and only deployment, a third of my platoon's marriages ended
in divorce. It's not an uncommon theme. But, of course,

with time, and luck, we all come to realize not only are we
Odysseus, we are Ajax and even the Cyclops, the whole lot—

the wooden horse, the Trojans, the arrow piercing the ankle.
We are all, in essence, Achilles's ambition. We are spring's last rain

watering a dandelion sprouting through a rock in a Cretan
olive grove. We are Paris and Helen before the invasion,

the late shift turning out as day breaks. We are the paddles
no longer swinging in middle school hallways, and we are the oars

sculling a wine-dark sea while mourners gather at the shore.
We are Poseidon and Athena—the final knock on the door.

Kickball Cowboy

One day in third grade, I grew tired of being picked last for kickball, so I showed up to school in a pair of faux leather cowboy boots my grandfather rescued from a dumpster. It worked. I was picked first and on my first attempt, my pointy boot hit that red rubber ball dead center, *doink*, into the outfield, *doink*, into Trey's face, *doink*, down the line. I scored six runs, leading to the annihilation of our opponents. If my teammates were strong enough, they would have carried me off the field. Alas, they, too, were only third graders, but they had their champion, and I had their love, at least until lunch, when my newfound fame would be usurped by the runny cheese of nacho day, but O, how I sat in the warm rays of victory, trying to memorize math tables, while Ms. Spelling took her secret nap. I wonder if she ever dreamt of robins pecking the earth that made us. Well, the making goes on, doesn't it? On the school bus home, my kickball cowboy dreams came to an end when I pissed off the wrong kid—two years older, mean daddy, called me a braggart. Admittedly, I did say I was the best kickball player in the state of Alabama. To this day, I have not been disabused of such a notion. However, on *that* day, Ricky, with his penny freckles, punched me many times. I lay there for what felt like an eternity within a somehow larger eternity (a nesting doll sort of nightmare). Finally, I kicked. I kicked and kicked and kicked again—pumping my legs like pistons in a souped-up, small block v8, which pissed off Ricky even more. I found my courage, sure, but he stripped me of both boots, and *whoosh*, out the window. Did I have it coming? Some of it, definitely, but my boots? I mean, they were two sizes too big, but think how many years' worth of home runs they had left! That's *all* I could think about at dinner, how it was just the beginning: me and those boots—all that room for my toes. Mom was beside herself: *He did what?* I told her I deserved it—*I was bragging*, I explained. *About what?* I was going pro. I'd have a celebration dance, endorsement deals, a condo on South Beach, wherever the hell that was. *James, what were you bragging about?* I shrugged, sore from the bruising. *Kickball*, I said.

Metaphysical Citrus

Always, it was *when*—a time marker
to begin. Never *how*, or *why*, until
the ending, perhaps. An epiphany
write from desperation, I might
challenge previous notions, then
introduce an image like *a woven basket
filled with oranges.* This tells me
nothing about why I am here. How
am I here, if not by the grace of
physics—the creation of pulp
no more than a particle wave
forming a sacred geometric
rhythm? I know it's about more
than simply clocking in. It takes
work to appreciate an orange basket.
To see the fruit flies as no more a
nuisance than the pesticides
hiding in the rind. It takes real work
to love what makes a thing a thing at all,
and time has very little to do with it.

The French Horn

In sixth grade, I knew little of France, even less of music, but O,
how I worshipped that marvel of coiled, mirrored brass.

I polished it with an old t-shirt each weekend.
Mother named it *Betsy, the fancy round trumpet.*

Mostly, I remember the buzz of each note on my lips
and how—when I forgot to breathe—I grew lightheaded;

the notes would leave the page, float like balloons from their staves
—*Think of them as the backbone*, our conductor said.

        I thought of them as ribs.

        Still, we watched her paint the air with a red baton;
    the flautist in the front row changed colors,
            her braided hair a wheat field in July,
        not a combine in sight,
            only clouds of watercolor
dribbling from a spit valve, the ping
            of the triangle settling somewhere
    between the slide of the trombone
            and the oboe's sigh,
        which is not unlike my mother's,
            when she tells me years later,
*I always wanted to play the saxophone,
        was handed a clarinet. The only song
    I learned was "Home on the Range."*
        When I asked, *How old were you?*
    She said, *Probably fifteen?*
        About a year before you were born.

All these years later,
and I'm losing my right hand
inside the horn's bell
—all of it disappearing: me,
Mother, the music.

The notes drop
like paper clips to the floor,
and I wonder, *What if
she'd been handed
a saxophone?*

I play it out measure by measure.
I see her in Tuscaloosa, graduating from the University of Alabama,
then moving to Birmingham—a social worker, a nurse,
a selfless refrain that ends with a violin's solo.

Since she told me, it's all I can see:
my pregnant, teenaged mother
holding a clarinet with a cracked reed,

me kicking her belly
like a bass drum, both of us
wanting the hell out of there.

Highway 45 Truck Stop

—Hamilton, Mississippi

It's simple. You scoop ice
into a bag. After you pack it tight,
you spin the bag at the neck,
then clamp the tie. You
carry each bag to the freezer
in front of the store. The monotony
keeps your body moving
in the early morning
before the farmers
sit in the window booths,
hawked over cups of coffee. They
speak loud enough
for you to catch phrases:
The cows are running free,
or, *She can't get pregnant*,
but there is no context, except
for the nickels tolling in your ears,
and for each bag of ice,
one falls into your pocket,
which is already filled with
so many nickels you don't know where
you'll put them. Maybe you'll buy
some music or shoes.
You won't. You never do.
The shoes you are wearing
are good enough for
the job, and later, there is
college, you hope, but
aren't sure, so you take the scoop
in your hand and thrust it
into ice. You spin the bag.
You clamp the tie.
There are many like you, but

you are still young,
and you tell yourself,
I won't get stuck. You
say it every day, until it happens.

Nine Persimmons

And he will shew you a large upper room furnished
and prepared: there make ready for us.
—Mark 14:15

You're at dinner with a friend, an artist, who has prepared eggplant parmesan
    with his mother,
who is Italian—who was kissed, as a girl, by Mussolini, who (it is rumored)
    admired persimmons

and ordered the public to plant their seeds in gardens and orchards—
    To feed the soldiers,
your artist friend says. Across from you, at the table,
    are nine persimmons

ripening on the sill, lined up like little round soldiers wearing green hats.
    Aren't they perfect? he says.
They are, you reply. *They are the most sincere fruit*, he says.
    When you ask,

Why do you say that? He says, *Look at them.* You do, while his mother
    recalls
what she heard in her youth. *To predict winter, farmers split open
    the seeds.*

If shaped like a fork, mild, if spoon, snow—knife, ice.
    You remember
your first bite of one—how it wasn't ready. It was, however, sincere.
    You fell to the ground,

your mouth puckering, drawing into itself, then you remember how
    the rest of you
followed—a "spoon and knife" kind of winter, huddled around a space heater
    in an unfinished house

with a can of potted meat and six saltines. *A fine dinner*, you thought to yourself,
    grateful for each bite.
Besides, there would be other winters, and, often, the milder ones
    hit hardest.

Sometimes loved ones disappeared for no reason, others
    for good reason,
then there's the one you *really* love who decided, last Christmas, to leave you,
    then changed her mind

—*I was confused*, she said. *I have loved you always*, she said.
    You divorce the following year.
But you're not there yet. No, you're eating dinner at your friend's house,
    and those persimmons

are ripening on the sill. She's sitting next to you, while your friend's mother
    explains all
you'll ever need to know about this fruit, and it's in this moment,
    fork and knife in hand,

napkin on your lap, when you realize you don't need to crack open a seed
    to predict what you
already know about winter, which is this: everyone will leave you,
    or you them,

and yes, it's dark—dark as the dead sun at the solstice,
    but you're grown now
and so is your wife. You've arrived at what you've both known all along,
    but couldn't see until now.

You begin to notice all sorts of things, the gingham tablecloth
    matching the curtains,
the bell on the mantle, the light at the dock.
    You notice

how your friend turned each persimmon just so. You even notice
    that part of you
feels the persimmons judging you from their sill, but you don't mind it.
    You eat well.

You share polite conversation. When you finish, you help clear the table,
    and when your wife
gives you the look that says, *It's time to go*, you say your goodbyes,
    and your friend

hands each of you a persimmon for the road. In the car, before you pull off,
    your wife says, *I've never eaten a persimmon*,
and neither have you—not ripe. Not like this. So you eat them right then and there.
    You smile the whole ride home.

After the Rain

Robins everywhere—in the trees,
on the ground, scratching at the leaves for bugs,

rejoicing, and above, the white eye,
slow to blink, is full

and shining between two pines,
where a banana spider restrings her web,

which is her story—every thread,
but there's more here than mere story.

There are robins in the birdbath, on the roof
—a shrill song filling the high ceilings

of early morning, where revelation
is a flash of red breast and two black coins for eyes

calling out—calling out with all its breath for a mate,
for sunrise, for the camellias to bloom.

Winter in Georgia

Imagine a story that doesn't end
and you're halfway there.
Imagine having a friend who loves the word doom
—especially the *m*, which closes the mouth,
Like a period, she says.
Imagine she also loves the name, Carl,
having never met a Carl.

Imagine she likes how the *a* stretches out
like a spring between the *c* and the *r*,
and how the *r* and the *l*
weld the name shut. I like to imagine
she meets a Carl who loves her
as much as she loves *Gone with the Wind*.
Clark Gable and Vivien Leigh

—a story that, in her mind, doesn't end
when Rhett walks out on Scarlett,
a scene she unrolls
when she imagines an ending
where Rhett stays and they work things out,
then drive off into the sunset
in a black Cadillac, into a world

that hasn't left them behind.
Imagine it all happening on a winter day
in Georgia, where, outside the car,
it's snowing vowels over Atlanta,
and because Carl is in love,
he pulls the car over so she can get out
and catch the letters with her tongue.

The Alley

Let's say crime is the alley we ignore, a scratched-up mirror
on a coffee table, a junky door, and let's say Jesus
loved a prostitute, because he did, and let's say the small-town gangster
who, last night, popped three rounds from a semiautomatic pistol,

once loved his neighbor, the girl who kissed him
behind a curtain at the block party—how they both hid,
stared at each other in a cocoon of light, then panicked.
Knew it was wrong. They'd known it all their lives.

* * *

Can love be innocent? Can a kiss? They were kids.
Let's say we're all billions of years old, fumbling for light.
Let's say he loved her too—at least, in that moment
—that their hearts still wander back,

down that knock-kneed dumpster alley,
that you have your alleys too—yes, reader, you.
Let's say you've boxed your feelings. *Don't you dare*
ruin our good name. I hear it. Don't you know?

* * *

I know all of these lines. I wrote them as they wrote you.
And here, again, comes our hero,
burning through new tires outside my window,
popping his pistol—and why, I wonder? Why does the sun go on?

Why do we? What to do with all these boxes?
No bubble wrap either, just tossed in—a real mess.
How many times have you kissed and told?
Or not? Does this poem frighten you? It should.

* * *

But in the case that it doesn't, I'm sure you've heard rumors
of people you know well—good, hardworking people,

people you love, people like your friend who smokes
a little weed, but hides it, is ashamed,

knows you hate it, is afraid you'll cut him out,
or your sister, who snorts Adderall at lunch
to *Stay on the grind!* Or your mother-in-law, a widow
with a porn subscription and a vibrator, too!

* * *

My God! The shame! Stone her now!
Not to mention the omission.
How could they keep their lives hidden from you?
It's important to shield a newborn's eyes from too much light.

Even if the child isn't yours. Even if you can't accept
that your child isn't yours. It's not easy to accept,
which may be one reason for people not accepting it.
Maybe we need a mediator, a savior, a final commandment?

* * *

What was it he said? *Love one another?*
Where's the mention of ownership in those three words?
Property? We let in the moneylenders.
We let them name us. We let them rule us.

We, with our junky doors hanging from lusty hinges
that we just don't know how to fix—we appointed landlords and said, *Fix it!*
Name it! Then fix it! We know who owns both sides of the alley.
We know where our bread is buttered, don't we?

* * *

When I was a boy a woman with a feather boa visited our class.
She belly danced to Middle Eastern music,
shimmying like a grape vine between our cute little desks,
her coin belt flashing an ancient spell.

Near the end of her set, she stopped in front of me.
I was bewitched. She lassoed my neck

with her boa, and when she did, every part of me
rose up out of myself, my heart pumping with Greek fire,

* * *

a fire that would burn in me my whole life—for her, yes,
but for all the women who came after, who whispered wisdom
far and near, but it was she who was my savior, my Gaia,
my Mother Mary who raised me from the dead earth

and breathed life into my flesh, who showed me how to love and be loved
—that love is not a word *at all*, but a mystery
far from the world of shame or sin. *A heart*, she said,
cannot sin. And when she left, the other kids looked at me,

* * *

asked, *What did she say? Tell us*, they demanded.
I said nothing. For thirty years, I boxed her away, until now.
She's right. A heart cannot sin. You know this,
with your flashlight-under-the-covers,

pinup shame, your on-again, off-again crushes, midnight guilt,
stolen, melted candy bar–karma, your crushed-velvet seat,
chromed-out fantasies turning into the alley
for one last blow job behind the Circle K.

* * *

I, too, am in love with the world, with its many herbs,
its rhodiola and saffron, its bright cannabis stalks
growing tall in red-state basements, and I am in love with its prophets
who dance in classrooms where questions grow tomorrows

—the world a dervish with three holes whirling down
lane #3 at the local alley—alley of alleys.
Cue the greasy cheeseburger, the register, the aerosol shoe spray.
Pan to a high five, an usher clearing a table.

Sun & Moon

How is it a college dropout finds himself at a bluegrass concert
on a mountainside in southwest Virginia
wearing a lampshade for a top hat? It's raining

and Vince Gill's singing an a cappella rendering
of "Go Rest High on That Mountain"
and the mountain is listening—so too my grand projection,

Mr. Lampshade who's walking barefoot into the Porta-Potty,
knocking his "hat" onto the ground,
where it stays until he wobbles back out,

zips up his pants and, *How high do you think he is?*
my friend asks, leaning over the cooler. *High enough*

to wear a lampshade as a hat, I say.
He does sort of glow, she says. *Doesn't he?*

*

When I was barely old enough to speak, Mother says
I looked out the car window,
made a come-hither motion with my hand,
and said, *Come to me, Moon.*
Several years later it did, in a dream,
though it wasn't white like it is in the sky.
It was sort of like coal, but also like a pearl.

Songs swam around it like a school of seahorses
holding on to each other's tails.
When I woke, I'd write what I remembered
on the bus window with my finger.
I impressed a friend, Amy. She
blew me kisses, gave me a mix tape
with songs she recorded from the radio.

In her valentine, she wrote, *You're mine, always.*
She didn't know that I would soon move,
that *always* is not a word heard on the moon.

II

The Sun King

Louis XIV woke each morning to a window facing east, where a seventeenth-century sun affirmed his claim of divine right. At Versailles, the rooms have names like the War Room, the Peace Room, the Hall of Mirrors. Outside, the Orangery. Why is it I can never seem to finish the bag of oranges in the refrigerator? I, too, wake facing east, though no sun shines through my bedroom wall, and while I don't have a hall dedicated to mirrors, my modest 1950 ranch boasts two—each in a bathroom. They're the old lead ones. One of them is chipped on the corner. I try to remind guests to be careful around them. I'm sure Louis had the same problem when he invited nobles over to hunt and eat and drink and fuck—an honorable scheme, indeed, to keep them from slitting each other's throats, or worse, his. I'm sure he, too, owned a chair with a weak leg or a horse that never turned right. One must remember, all that glitters is not gold, though, in his case, much of it was. I haven't lived in the same place for more than a handful of years. He ruled for seventy-two, demanded Europe revolve around him as the planets revolve around the sun. That was the model, and doesn't it sound good? It always *sounds* good. Imagine yourself waking in the same place every day—everything revolving around you. Everything in its place because of you—the alarm, your kids, the laundry half folded in handed-down dresser drawers, and yes, even the stray that limps into your life at precisely the worst moment. Who walks into a king's life expecting nothing? Not so foreign now, is it? How could it be that I am as divine as he? Me, with no Orangery. Me, with my floppy house shoes, my weepy eye? How can it be that we are embers of a dying star, lighting up each morning to rule our tiny kingdoms, our workplace romances, our patches of fescue? Louis' *jardins* were the talk of Europe. Statues of Apollo competed with fountains and geometrically-designed paths leading into colonnades and lily pad ponds. I once saw an exhibit on prairie grasses at a botanical garden, and what I remember were the roots, stretched out like ancient rivers, no different than the Seine. The plaque said they grew as deep as fifteen feet—each root an anchor in a sea and all of it for a spindle in the sun—a blossom, a bee.

Changing a Truck Battery

The cables broke off in the teeth
of my channel locks, lead
terminal corroded worse than the tile floor
at Steak 'n Shake, where they
still haven't found a decent recipe
for hash browns. Anyway, I shocked

the ever-loving shit out of myself,
forgetting to remove the negative before
the positive, frying three fuses—
one of which controls my power steering pump,
and yes, it was all easy enough to fix,
and no, I didn't get hurt too bad,

save the weird jaw pain
that seemed to come out of nowhere,
which probably had more to do
with dehydration than my world-renowned
mechanical talents, but what do I do
with a locked jaw, a fifteen-year-old pickup,

and this angst I haven't felt
since before this truck was built?
Where do I haul it? Upon
whose outstretched arms, whose cross
do I hang it? Why would I
want to give away such grief so easily,

when I can toss it in the bed,
pop the clutch, and coast down the hill
for coffee with an old friend? I love Jesus.
I also love commiserating
with those who don't have a prayer—
who struggle, like me, with praying at all.

Coal

By now, I know better
than to run my mouth around my cousins
who wake every day in a place
called Pig-Shit Alley,
who descend a mile-deep
shaft for black lung
and a disappearing pension.

We all get taken,
sure, but who takes from a widow?
Who drinks the well's last
dregs, the backwash,
the swallowed, the spit-back
and forgotten? What help
is there for the woman

who's lost every man
she's ever loved to a company
she's never seen?
Click, click, go the numbers
on the dial. *Click, click*,
go the executive's *Florsheims*
into the never-ending

expanse of industry
spackled over with marble and stained oak
—a boardroom painted canary yellow.
Truth is hard to find,
especially when all you've got
is a headlamp and a pick.
But the lights—they do flicker.

They shine like hell
until they finally burn out.

Mississippi Snow

He drives up from Biloxi to talk about working at the shipyard. *We've got our own rules down there*, he says, then whips out his phone to show me UFOs he filmed off his dock. Three lights dip and swerve in all sorts of ways I've never seen. Then, as if someone had stumbled behind the curtain and flipped a switch, the lights go off. *They're here, man. I see them all the time. Who knows how long they've been visiting us. Who do you think built the pyramids? The Egyptians*, I say. He looks at the floor, shakes his head—*well, how do you explain that video? Don't you believe me?* I look at him with all the tenderness I have, say, *Of course, I do. Would you like to go outside?* We migrate to the backyard, where Orion is still suspended in space—his arrow condemned to its bow. Our eyes adjust to the dark. *The shipyards are like cities—each boat a skyscraper turned on its side.* I ask him how long he's chewed tobacco. *Since the beginning*, he says. He leans against the grill, talks about dry docks and spillways, the year he roughnecked offshore, catching goliath groupers, then, after eating them, dropping their bones back to the deep. He doesn't drink anymore, chicken biscuit for breakfast, keeps his truck on half a tank. *I only fill it all the way when I'm headed out of town.* The moon floats in the pool like a paper plate. Two frogs croak on the sliding glass door. *It's a grind, man. Some days I don't know how much longer I can go on. There's this fella who's been working the yard for thirty-five years—no sign of retiring—crane operator—climbs that ladder every morning. Takes everything with him: his lunch cooler for what goes in and a bucket for what comes out.* We walk off the porch and into a cotton field—stroll each row like ships cutting a channel. *Mississippi snow*, he says, then bends down and carefully draws a ball from its thorny clutch, touches it to his tongue. *Doesn't melt though, does it? No it doesn't*, I say, and by now we're both feeling a little hungry and headed to Waffle House, where we find ourselves talking over coffee and tall cups of water. *We sure can talk, can't we?* And that's it. We pay up and go back to our lives. We meet back up several years later, then a few more after that, and it always ends the same. Our stories stack like leftovers in the fridge.

Refrain

there is a song
and in it my boyhood self

walks home apples
ripening in brown sacks

two cans of knockoff
butterbeans a runny

nose and a shoe
in need of mending

*

there is a song
no guitar can play

and it sounds like flour
sifted over a pan like lightning

never leaving a cloud
a lover who never speaks

too loud it hums like lips
on the skin of a drum

The Minister of Macaroni

—after Wallace Stevens

At ten years old, I'd say he's *quite* accomplished
switching on the burner, following directions
on the back of the box, the water
rising to a boil, how he stands
on a chair to drop in the macaroni,
then it's two hands on the handle
and *big muscles* to the colander
waiting in the sink. Strain. Noodles
back to the pot. Stir in the mix. *A real dinner*,
he thinks to himself as he dishes out portions
for his brother and sister who are waiting
at the table, bowls in their hands.

My Younger Self Attempts Breakdancing
at the Sadie Hawkins Dance

I spin like an adolescent bottle
pointing in empty directions,

the colors of the divided gym
spiraling like one of Mrs. Peters's

chemistry experiments, the blurry girls
staring, the boys huddled together

like cows in a thunderstorm.
A minute ago, I sensed the movement,

two Samanthas on their way to our side
with their rare request.

Would you like to . . . ?
But I wasn't waiting. I'd have my say first.

Now, I listen for the beat to drop
and I pose, balancing

all my weight on my left hand,
each leg a limp karate kick.

I move as a squid flees
a cameraman's light,

arms crawling like
honeysuckle along a trellis.

If I love my body,
if any of us love our bodies,

we don't know it yet.
What I *do* know?

When I loop and coil
on the hardwood, my limbs

flex like sound waves,
as if I could speak for the air,

as if, right now, I am all
I will ever be, popping and locking

like some postmodern
dubstep magician,

which I am, in this moment,
oblivious, for once, of my blasphemous

body, spinning into a world all its own,
until, finally, the faces unblur

as before, and I see a smile from a name
I will not remember,

her hand reaching out to pick my bones
from the polished floor.

Heat Index

Summer, but not cantaloupe-ripe summer,
not tomato-ripe, not watermelon-ripe,
not making love with the windows open,
riding downtown at midnight
with the top down, radio blaring
another teenage pop sensation
too-bland-to-be-offensive summer.

No, it's a burnt sod, thunderstorm summer.
Don't lie to me! It's a World Cup summer.
*Don't lie to yourself, Son. Get up
and drink that Dr. Pepper.* Another
bullets in the street summer.
Another blood-hot, angry Apollo
chasing the ice cream truck with a buck

for a *Popsicle* kind of summer. When
the walk gives way to dandelions,
gives way to Charlie Chaplin,
then Charlie Murphy walks into Tick Tock Tavern,
and what? *Want a punch line, Punk?*
You're only smiling because you're scared.
The kind of summer that makes you

beg for winter kind of summer.
That fear-riddled mangy dog summer,
and don't the butterfly weed
smell like petunias to a dirty-minded Monarch?
Go on and tip your crown into the lake.
Break your heel on cobblestone
in Savannah. Hold your phone

up like an antenna and call
down your angels like the God you are.

You hear Dizzy's trumpet
blaring like an homage to Jericho?
You hear them walls collapsing?
You see the pig's middle split wide,
smell that vinegar? Better grab a rib

before the meat has a chance to rest.
Carolina may be calling, but
I've got work in the morning,
and my ancestors didn't leave me
nothing but a bad back.
Summer-job summer. Dried-up riverbank,
records warped like tortillas spinning

like curveballs over homes filled
with teenagers in love. We're all obvious
and ignorant, but don't tell us.
Don't ask us to look at something we
fully understand. We've got Sheetrock
to hang and floors to hammer in.
I peel the same callous each night before bed.

The Man in the Bucket

Isn't he a sight, this sunburned baloney bender
two days from vacation, this hungry lineman
who forgot his lunch, this recovering alcoholic with a meeting tonight,
this father who never knows what to say, who takes a pill
for the anxiety that starts in his chest, spreads to his hands,
this endless electricity, these cables and leg irons, this joy jelly
for the elbows, and don't they creak something awful?

What I wouldn't give for a cherry picker view,
to live life in a bucket, hanging by a wire, the kid back home,
a game I can't make, the argument, the resentment,
the makeup conversation ten years later—after the kid grows up,
gets a job, understands—to have a trade to ply and pass on?
It's romantic, no? To me, he's almost a fighter pilot.
We're up to our eyeballs in shit. He's up there giving us light.

The Beehive

High up in the water oak, nestled
  into a hollow piece of trunk,
    a beehive glowing like the sun
    —the workers buzzing in and out,
landing with their full sacs—
      all pomp and beeswax.

Down here it's three wet logs
  and more smoke than fire,
    this mosquito-thick evening
    sponsored by Budweiser's latest
nonalcoholic beer. Sobriety
      tastes warm and flat,

but dripping down the trunk,
  a thread of sticky gold
    catches the final ashes of dusk,
    and I have the thought
to grab the ladder from the garage
      and rob them,

but it's late and the fire's dying down.
  Also, I don't own
    a beekeeping suit with the fancy hood
    and veil, the three layers of mesh.
I'm not my great-grandfather
      who kept bees

and raised hogs while raising
  children and winning
    local checkers events.
    Remember playing checkers?
Remember saying, *King me?*
      then stacking two stones

and twisting them to completion
　　—the satisfying *bite*
　　　of the plastic teeth,
　　then the triple jump to win?
No, I'm afraid I'll not be
　　　　robbing the bees tonight.

Tooth of the Lion

I am walking the dog in dandelion season
and I am worried about my neighbor,
who has surgery next week. I pray for him,
but he does not believe in prayer. I am
walking the dog in dandelion season
and the sun is setting beyond the hill

and Merlin, the dog, my sweet comrade,
wants to swallow it all. He is lunging
at a squirrel that always seems to escape.
The dogwood is a glittering, golden coin.
My mother is calling me. I am not answering.
I am walking the dog. The neighborhood

has yet to mow the grass: dandelions
and wildflowers everywhere: shamrocks
and spiderwort, clover and jasmine
—from patio to driveway—a pastel paradise
for a week. The neighbor is having surgery
next week. I pray, but he does not believe.

Why do I not answer the phone? *Call me,*
she says on the voicemail. *It's not important,*
she says, *I just miss you.* I miss her too,
but my sweet comrade must walk.
It is all he wants in this world—to smell
these flowers in this light on this day,

and I *will* call my mother. I *will.* Later,
I will tell her of work. She will talk about
the mountains, a log cabin; I will listen,
knowing I will miss her more and more
with time, then I will miss her entirely.
Honestly, I have never seen so many dandelions.

Self-Portrait as Peach Orchard

By orchard, I mean one peach tree
in late March, rosy blossoms
fanning out in a yard at the edge of town,
where a retired couple weary of leftovers
hands the pizza delivery driver
a check which he cannot take.
They pay cash, undertip,
fold their soggy slices, eat. One
blames the other. They promise to make
better choices for the rest of the week.
That evening, the *other*
makes the Ben & Jerry's run.
By self-portrait, I mean associative
dissonance.

    I mean a handful of ibuprofen
after running no more than two miles
this morning, the neighborhood's mowers
all firing up at once to celebrate
my return to fitness, to cut
the first bright burst of spring.

       Adieu, petites violettes.
       So long, aster and crocus,
       primrose, trout lily.

       Greetings, pothole and
       subsequent ankle sprain.

       Pace e bene, whispers the relief
       of St. Francis stuck
       to the medicine cabinet.

       *

Later, green sky, streaks of gray
—pink bolts flash and fork.

Rain for days and the ditch kitties
with nowhere to go. They

swish their tails, blink
into parallel universes, eat

salmon from marble bowls
in tall-windowed, pillowy mansions.

They dream of mice
wearing bow ties,

and when the ditches
finally drain, they lick their paws

and blink back
to their culvert kingdoms.

*

Perhaps it's the uniformity
that lends credibility to an orchard,
the straight lines in every direction.

Still, I prefer *Der einsame Baum*,
the lone tree in a field
stretching for light.

By peach, I mean what remains
after eating—the few strands
of flesh left clinging to the stone.

III

Manatee

I just got off the phone with my eighty-six-year-old grandmother, with whom I spent half an hour comparing weed eater brands. It sounded like she was talking about God the whole time—that God is somehow the string *and* the spool, even the handle, that *we* are the hands. I'm okay with God being the string *or* the spool, maybe even the hands? Well, according to my grandmother, were God to pick a weed eater, it'd be a Toro. I didn't tell her I own a Craftsman, or that I haven't weed-eated in a month. It's bad enough I waited so long to call. Who knows, maybe time is one fractal in a chain of fractals. Aren't we all the same tree? Isn't a Craftsman as much a Toro as a Toro is a manatee? *It's about the quality!* she says. What about the sea cow? I feel like I'm losing the thread, but doesn't it all break down eventually? *Pay a little more up front—sticks around longer*, she says. And when she says it, I dismiss the manatees altogether and think of all the time she's poured into me—all the ass-whoopings, lectures, and hot cocoa. I never once saw her lose at badminton. I thought for years she was on a well. Nope, city water. *Brilliant's got the best water in the county!* She's right. It's the coal in the ground. Here, in my neighborhood, the water tastes like mud. Here, I spend time in the yard to remind me of her, which reminds me of her mother and all the mothers before her. Their voices gather like water in the trumpet vine ascending the loblolly. *My child*, I hear, and I'm there, in my grandmother's yard where my brother tackles me, full throttle into a holly bush—both of us barefoot and shirtless, our sunburned skin pierced by spiky medieval leaves. Afterward, we drink a gallon of sweet tea, feel proud of our bruises and blood. *Time catches us all*, says the trumpet vine, and maybe it all *doesn't* break down eventually. Maybe the hawk that just landed in the red oak isn't *just* a hawk. Maybe a conversation about weed eaters is as close as I'll ever get to talking with God, but how lucky am I to be in rural Georgia   in a place that reminds me of her, where it's peanuts and Coca-Cola with a sprinkling of New Testament—a Jesus who sounds like ambrosia salad: *Verily, verily I say unto you, butter your popcorn heavily, salt it well, then toss, for the dessert of heaven is not born of sugar, but of grain.* I hear you, Jesus! Verily, verily I hear it, and when I do, there I am, again, BB in my leg, pumping an air rifle—another feudal dispute with my brother. We hide behind trees, *Peek-a-boo!* Fire. Then, the yelp, the story at school the next day, the argument over who told it better. There sails another memory, the last of it flickering off a candy wrapper in the ditch. *You need to take better care of the yard*, blares the trumpet vine. Would you look at that! There goes the hawk to make another cloud.

My Unborn

You enter through the side door I leave open,
flurry in on little white petals from the tea olive.

You smell like ripe apricots. It's a quiet,
forgiving Saturday morning. Even the dog

is quiet, curled into himself like a cloud
—all of it Your gift, I know. I'm curled up too,

having woken from the cruel dream.
A dream You gave me only moments ago

—the same dream that enters like You,
like always, like wind through a spent chrysalis

—a hollow rattling, the echo of my unborn.
In the dream she's all song, playing

with a bluebird that flies around her head,
lands in her hands. She's wearing a yellow dress,

white shoes. When I wake, and
she's not there, the empty sits in me

like iron in a mountain. Still, I open the door,
hoping it's she who'll come running in

all a flurry with her bird, her song, her white shoes
the white petals of the tea olive—her hair

the ripe apricots, but it's never her, Lord.
Like everything else, it's You—all of it.

In the dream the bluebird sings her name.
I can never remember what it is.

Pulchrum est Paucorum Hominum

Once upon a time, a girl grew up wanting
—more than anything else—to see the Eternal City.

For years she asked her father to take her,
but he only replied, *Nullo modo est in inferno!*

She dreamt of sunlight seeping into cobblestone
while she pushed a toy cart along the grain

of the kitchen table, carved statuettes
applauding her entry through imaginary gates.

Their faceless welcome warmed her on winter nights,
then, as if one of those statues had sprung to life,

her father burst through the door after a plentiful season
and told his daughter, *Eamus romam!*

She packed a satchel of clothes, stuffed her toys
into her pockets, and off they went

on a three-day trip to the seat of Italy's heart.
A wayward seafarer loitering outside a tavern

begged her father for a denarius,
which he gave in exchange for a better route.

Her father spoke of great Romans.
His favorite: Cincinnatus, who, no longer

needed as consul, returned to his cottage and plow.
On the last day of their journey, the buggy wheels

snagged and bumped on the old road,
and with each knock a figurine fell from her pocket,

bouncing behind and falling into cracks and crags,
but how could she notice what she'd lost along the way,

when Rome and its gleaming soldiers
stood before her, the fish markets alive with the reek

of the Tiber, fabrics of every shade and texture
waving her further into mysteries she'd never

imagined? And, O! The columns that stretched
their long necks, and how those necks caught the light!

Nectarine

Each bite brings you closer
to a beginning that has yet to begin,
and why you keep eating
has little to do with how juicy
or sweet it tastes. Since
a child you were taught to finish
what you start, and this,
like your job, like your marriage,
the laundry reeking
in its cloth bag—it's easier
to finish a nectarine. Besides,
with time, the big things
end themselves, and
like this nectarine, if left alone,
it will rot on the tree. But
if you pick it when it's ripe?
If you put it to your sunburned lips—

Field

Knotted cedar posts strung with barbed wire,
   red barn sitting like Vishnu
at the center of a mandala
   shaped like a temple. Inside,
a cow slurps water. Four stomachs
   churn grass into milk,
then the heart's electric pump
   vibrates the whole to set the field
in a perfect motion of stillness.
   The farmer walks between strokes
of a celestial paintbrush,
   is a dollop of rose-white paint
drifting toward the western gate,
   corn bucket swinging
from her right hand. The gate opens
   onto a gravel road. The road
leads to a small town with a Phillips 66,
   where high school kids park cars
and resolve the beginnings of their lives.
   Here is the heaven of *Paradisio*.
Here, the churning of grass
   into milk and milk into butter.
Here is the water pulled from the well,
   the wrinkle in the wallpaper,
and the farmer's belly sigh
   when she sees the fence
downed by either rot or intent,
   which means the long walk back
to the pickup to grab steel post and driver,
   a pair of pliers and a bit of wire.
Then it's the work of driving the post,
   stringing the fence. It's the making
of a universe and its undoing.

The High Priestess

—Rider-Waite Tarot Deck

is not as well-read as she'd have you believe,
but she looks the part in a blue robe,

sun passing through a pair of longhorns,
the moon at her feet, cross on her chest,

pillars at each side, curtain of pomegranates
draped behind her, and beyond that,

a lake, land, sky. She looks straight ahead,
unmoved, one hand hidden in her robe,

the other holding the Torah. There's power
in the appearance of being well-read.

She knows veils better than most
—is a veil herself sitting in the portal,

her parole officer waiting at Denny's,
his stack of pancakes growing cold.

She joins him as soon as the artist
finishes coloring her in. When she arrives,

she notices the officer's new haircut.
She likes it, but keeps it to herself.

Besides, she thinks he's too quiet—all business.
Why don't you trust me? she whispers,

then watches the busser stack mugs
and plates in a plastic bin. His answer

seems to float out of his mouth like a fat bee.
She thinks how she'd love to be a spoon

in that bin, face turned upside-down,
inside-out, to feel the spray of hot suds

in the dishwasher—to be sanitized, dried,
but she has months to go, and *Mr. Business*

seems annoyed with her daydreaming.
I want to trust you, I do, he says. *Then trust me*,

she says, *Just because I'm not like you
doesn't mean I want to burn down the city.*

Help me then, he says. She drinks her coffee,
says, *Okay, imagine having the moon*

as a guest in your home. That's against policy,
he says, *also, it doesn't make sense.*

Yes it does, she says, *now, look me in the eye,
and tell me a story—begin with the middle,*

then lose your way. I'm not a storyteller,
he says. *Neither is the moon*, she says.

Maria

At seven, I ate my first *real* banana in the Azores, a volcanic archipelago of nine islands bubbled up like soap suds in the middle of the Atlantic. It was always windy and the bread tasted sweet. But on this one particular morning in spring, I walked into the backyard of a cottage where we were staying—my family and me; I remember walking down a stone path into a small banana orchard, then reaching up on my tippy-toes and pulling one down, ripe, then walking over to a rock wall, happy as I'd ever be. As I sat there, pushing my hair out of my eyes, I peeled the banana with such care, one might have thought I'd discovered the first fruit. There I sat, seven years old, eating a banana on a rock wall near the edge of a caldera while two peacocks paraded by, squawking, batting their eyelashes. The landlady saw me, asked if I'd had breakfast, *Essas bananas são boas, não? Mas você já comeu seus ovos?* She was short, like me. Her name was Maria, like the Maria from church, and she had curly black hair, a kind voice, but scarred—a voice like smoke, like she spent a few years singing in back alley Fado bars in Coimbra, then her mother got sick and she had to come home, stayed. Maria took my hand, and off we went to the big house, which wasn't all that big. She said my parents were coming over as well. They did. We sat in wooden folding chairs on a veranda overlooking the orchard, which looked as if it were waving—all those leaves in the wind. The peacocks, she said, were her mother's. Her mother hated them, she said. I told her I loved them, and she said I was young, and to eat as many bananas as I wanted.

Buffalo Rock

Ten miles south of Fayette, Alabama,
    a rock shaped
    like a Buffalo stands

somewhere in a thicket
    off a dirt road.
    My great-grandmother

described how it was carved
    by lightning.
    She remembered the ground

speaking. Before she died, I
    packed a lunch,
    and each weekend

for a month, I went
    looking for it.
    Buffalo Rock, she called it,

though she must have been lying,
    because I never found
    the rock, but you and I know

the only thing that matters
    is the rock,
    the rock and the field

around it. We misconceive
    myth: a world
    inside a world inside a world

—a place so quiet, it fails
    to be heard,
    like a song poured from a jar.

The Wayne C. Henderson Music Festival, Grayson Highlands State Park

—for James Kimbrell

If a guitar ever fell from heaven, it'd be found on the Crooked Road.
To get there, we climb through Georgia,
where it takes six orange helmets

to fill a pothole. Call it Cracker Barrel
paradise, gravy bowls on every table.
After four hours of traffic it's on to Zebulon.

Our chariot is a quad cab Toyota
with mud tires, and for every Peterbilt
there's a bear claw of a man

sticky with peach juice cocking a .357
named Ol' Betty. She waits in the glove box
for some lucky *sumbitch* stupid enough to come knocking.

After thumping each tire with a baseball bat,
I ask Jimmy, our captain, if he'd ever bungee jump
from a cellphone tower. He says the universe

is the internet squared. I must be
its orphan, looking at three massive crosses
broken like French fries on a ragweed-dusted mountain.

The Blue Ridge is a wrinkled quilt laid over a clothesline,
bluegrass on every station, each string picked clean,
fingers on the fret, and I'm old enough

to know God loves E minor more than D.
When we arrive, Wayne C. Henderson's holding
a guitar he's been working on for a year.

Jimmy asks for it and starts playing.
He picks every song he's ever learned in a mad dash
for sudden fame, then like a man possessed,

tosses the plastic and starts fingerpicking like a Carter.
O! Captain! My Captain! How many pilgrimages
must a man make to reach Jerusalem?

We've been here before, but when?
Perhaps, when these songs played on twangy Stellas,
when tent revival preachers wheezed through Leviticus

and the assured Second Coming of our Lord
and Savior—Jesus Christ Almighty
what good turnip greens! *Pass the pepper sauce!*

Even here, where charged air sparks
beneath a thunderhead, where blue-hairs
prod their husbands to swing them one last time,

> *When I soar to worlds unknown,*
> *See Thee on Thy judgment throne,*
> *Rock of Ages, cleft for me,*
> *Let me hide myself in Thee.*

"Fantastic Pelicans Arrive"

In Dave Smith's poem, "Fantastic Pelicans Arrive," the speaker refers to pelicans
    as "middle-aged monks." I love this reverent nod,
  this austere prayer ending the poem.
      John Donne comes to mind, as does John Milton.
    So many Johns!
      Mind you, I'm not a monk,
          but I do love to read books and work in the garden,

        so it may come
        as no surprise
        that I somewhat identify
        with monks,
        which may also be part
        of the reason why,
        when I remember
        "middle-aged monks,"
        I flash on a memory
        where I am walking
        The Met Cloisters
        in Washington Heights,
        New York.
           Coincidentally,
        I also flash
        on the poem,
        "Fantastic Pelicans Arrive,"
        when I find myself
        visiting castles,
        which is rare,
        but not as rare
        as one might think!

What I believe I am saying is, I love how poems
  so often seem like carousels
    spinning cotton candy,
      while pineapples grow kitten tails.

What's that? A red candle
weeping? A wedding gown?

How many swords are too many?
How many coins?

I may have been a little high the day I walked The Met Cloisters,
    but I do remember
  the famous unicorn tapestries—some of them
    showing a unicorn completely free,
      innocent as William Blake
        holding a shield in the coliseum.

Others showed a sad, ensnared unicorn.

O, there are a few in-between scenes,
spears and daggers, a lute melody

riding a current of daffodils into a bright,
yellow sunset that sounds like it tastes,

but what I hear most is the cry
of the villagers, the ropes, the ignorance.

*

What isn't electric? All of it flashing at once—Queen Elizabeth's emblem:
    the pelican piercing its breast
  to feed its young. I flash to Jesus—whose image
hangs by tiny nails upon crucifixes
    at each doorway of my home.

I'm cooking dinner. I'm pulling weeds.
    The monk, remember?
        I'm thinking of all the crosses
stained and rotting (or sprouting!) around the world,
    then, all the pelicans,

all the churches, all the organs
sounding off at once,
    bells ringing en masse.

        Also, if Jesus can be a pelican,
        why not a scared unicorn

        corralled into a fence,
        then poked at with long sticks,

        this poor mistranslated unicorn
        mangled by a dusty, medieval mob,

        then hung on a wall in a castle
        on a hill in New York City

        overlooking the Hudson River,
        which is now a toxic estuary?

Anyway, I don't usually go on like this (I do), but occasionally,
    one *must* call attention
        to a title like "Fantastic Pelicans Arrive."

        Do they ever!

For instance, picture me: I'm on a dock in Missouri looking at a squadron of
pelicans overtake another, much larger dock, the kind of dock that belongs
to someone who can afford to hire an electrician to install a light fixture. See,
for me, the pelican looks more like a middle-aged dinosaur than a monk, but,
if I look closely, the pelican's neck might pass for the robe of St. Francis, who
fits here, because he preached to birds. Still, I have to *really* think about it, and
when I do, I'm almost always thrown to the Belvoir Castle of my youth,

        where I'm walking the grounds in my favorite shoes;
            I look up and watch a hot air balloon
            rise with the sun over a dewy wheat field.

What am I saying? I've mentioned the sun twice, not once, the moon.
    The Jesus of Missouri
  may not be the Jesus of New Orleans,
    with its tall ceilings
      and Tarot readers,
  its Voodoo shops, its bar bathrooms
  guarded by trios of gossips.

      There may be no moon in your church.

    The Jesus of Missouri
      may not be a unicorn
      hemmed in by an illiterate village

armed with pitchforks,
      may not be a middle term
      in a card table spat.

Your Jesus may not
      be mine any more
      than your grandmother's

cornbread recipe is hers.
      What is it about cornbread
      and the New Testament?

Must be the lard, the iron skillet,
      the spray of Preacher's saliva
      collecting in the front row.

Our Jesus may not be a unicorn in The Met Cloisters or the pelican on the
    Louisiana state flag,
  or even these pelicans landing,
just now, in the Hudson River, the Lake of the Ozarks,
    or somewhere you've just gone,
      migrating to only-God-knows-where—

may not be my feet
(or yours) testing
this warm water,
but, truly, how fantastic
—wings spread wide—

the arrival.

The Peninsula

—Downtown Charleston

It's late in the day. A tourist pushes a stroller
over pea gravel in White Point Garden
    beneath a canopy of live oaks. Offshore,
    a Carolina sky threatens The Battery,
      the rows of concrete-filled Civil War cannons
      anchored by steel bolts, their sights fixed on the bay,
on thunderheads unfurling like the rotting sails
    of long-sunken ghost ships. Waves

    slap the seawall. Palms tip their crowns,
signaling the advance. What has become of spring?
    This park, with its relics, its monuments
    of men lifting rifles to God, to forgotten
    constellations? Mossy benches collect what's left
    of the living: sack lunches, people napping.
And what to make of this butterscotch sun,
    all of us unwrapped, burning? What of

    the azalea blossoms abandoning their branches?
They gather and whirl on gusts of salty air,
    rush down cobblestone, a blue sky
    growing darker—chimney-smoke clouds
    lingering over King Street, Church Street
    —the *front* marked by a stray scarf caught on a lamppost.
Where has it come from? It flaps like a guidon
    in the cloistered garden of a lemon-crème

    Colonial, where a dogwood stands sentinel,
wrought iron everywhere, birds assembling
    in the eaves—us, too. Clap of thunder.
    Another and another, then Charleston
    retreats into itself, into restaurants, museums,
    the City Market—the sea's howl shuddering

the sailboats huddled in the marina,
    roped-off and restless—all of us

    gazing out windows belonging to other people,
to families we'll never meet, banks
    and businesses—each of us desperate
    for petrichor, for the dry streets we walked
    only moments ago, for the silence that descends
    after the rain—when the sky splits and the sun
removes its gray cloak to resume its station
    robed in splendor, a coat of many colors.

Medieval Meditation

If you give an apple
to the sun, then ask for payment,
if the song in your living room
is the crack in the plaster,
the turn of the spoke,
the alphabet of a language
you don't know,
then maybe the throw pillow's disgust
is meant to remind you
of a previous life
—one where you stole
cherries from the market,
proposing to Saturday on Tuesday,
then staring up at stained glass
on Sunday, only to misread
the narrative—to decide,
instead, to focus
on the torch that soldered
green shards of glass
to resemble a crown. You stare
into the fire. Then you feel it,
the red lion prowling
in your chest, then the priest
sighs into the microphone,
and for the first time
in your life, you know this
is the last time you turn the other cheek,
taking the hand of your child,
whose belief—still green—
stands amazed by the gold-trimmed
robes swinging incensed prayers,
and you remember that word
from a class in high school

—*indulgences*, and when you hear it,
something like a bell rings
in the rafters, then reverberates
like cold water over your ribs.

Holy

Before light, a ruin,
   a cellar, a voice
in a photograph
   silenced by a crease,

then an unfolding,
   a stillness, rain,
a house at dawn,
   a couple standing

beneath a blue
   window, a memory,
a river beginning
   again and again

—an orchard
   before harvest.

      *

Then, harvest.
   Then, what's left:
a quilt, a lover,
   another story lost

in a field—a crow,
   a cloud unraveling,
morning breeze
   freeing the last

of the daffodils
   —a few pine cones
shaking loose,
   cracked open

on the ground,
   a *whenever*, a door.

Source Acknowledgments

I'd like to thank the editors of the following literary magazines in which these poems originally appeared or are forthcoming, some in slightly different versions:

The American Poetry Review: "Kickball Cowboy" & "Self-Portrait as Peach Orchard"
Cagibi: "The Sun King"
Colorado Review: "Metaphysical Citrus"
The Common: "Maria"
The Cortland Review: "Refrain"
The Crab Orchard Review: "The Alley," "Fantastic Pelicans Arrive," "Manatee," "My Unborn," "The Beehive," and "The Peninsula"
diode: "Nectarine"
The Florida Review: "The High Priestess"
Hampden-Sydney Review: "Medieval Meditation" and "Pulchrum Est Paucorum Hominum"
Kenyon Review Online: "Highway 45 Truck Stop"
The Missouri Review Online: "The World"
New Letters: "Nine Persimmons," "The French Horn," and "Photograph | Boy in Window"
New Ohio Review: "Heat Index" and "My Younger Self Attempts Breakdancing at the Sadie Hawkins Dance"
Poet Lore: "Coal"
Rhino: "A Bit of Luck," "Tooth of the Lion," and "The Wayne C. Henderson Music Festival, Grayson Highlands State Park"
Sugar House Review: "Field" and "Holy"
Sycamore Review: "Changing a Truck Battery"
Tampa Review: "Buffalo Rock"
The Tusculum Review: "The Heavens Opened, and God Said"
Willow Springs: "Mississippi Snow"

I wish to express particular gratitude to Alice Friman, Rodney Jones, James Kimbrell, Travis Mossotti, Kerry Beth Neville, and Laura Newbern, without whom this book would not exist. I'd also like to thank all my dear colleagues, editors, family, friends, readers, and teachers—to whom I am grateful.

Thanks to Carolyn Forche, whose workshop generated an early draft of "Holy."

"The Man in the Bucket" is for my brother, Justin Evans, and "Nine Persimmons" is for Peter Selgin.

And gratitude to the National Endowment for the Arts and Sewanee Writers' Conference whose fellowships allowed much-needed time and resources when writing these poems.

Backwaters Prize in Poetry

2024   Kimberly Ann Priest, Wolves in Shells
          Honorable Mention: Kerry James Evans, Nine Persimmons

2023   Julie Choffel, *Dear Wallace*
          Honorable Mention: Brandel Franco de Bravo, *Locomotive Cathedral*

2022   Laura Reece Hogan, *Butterfly Nebula*
          Honorable Mention: Henrietta Goodman, *Antillia*

2021   Laura Bylenok, *Living Room*
          Honorable Mention: Sophie Klahr, *Two Open Doors in a Field*

2020   Nathaniel Perry, *Long Rules: An Essay in Verse*
          Honorable Mention: Amy Haddad, *An Otherwise Healthy Woman*

2019   Jennifer K. Sweeney, *Foxlogic, Fireweed*
          Honorable Mention: Indigo Moor, *Everybody's Jonesin' for Something*

2018   John Sibley Williams, *Skin Memory*

2017   Benjamín Naka-Hasebe Kingsley, *Not Your Mama's Melting Pot*

2016   Mary Jo Thompson, *Stunt Heart*

2015   Kim Garcia, *drone*

2014   Katharine Whitcomb, *The Daughter's Almanac*

2013   Zeina Hashem Beck, *To Live in Autumn*

2012   Susan Elbe, *The Map of What Happened*

2004   Aaron Anstett, *No Accident*

2003   Michelle Gillett, *Blinding the Goldfinches*

2002   Ginny MacKenzie, *Skipstone*

2001   Susan Firer, *The Laugh We Make When We Fall*

2000   David Staudt, *The Gifts and the Thefts*

1999   Sally Allen McNall, *Rescue*

1998   Kevin Griffith, *Paradise Refunded*

The Backwaters Prize in Poetry was suspended from 2005 to 2011.

To order or obtain more information on these or other University of Nebraska Press titles, visit nebraskapress.unl.edu.